50 Smoked Salmon and Fish Dishes

By: Kelly Johnson

Table of Contents

- Smoked Salmon Eggs Benedict
- Smoked Salmon and Avocado Toast
- Smoked Salmon Pasta with Cream Sauce
- Smoked Salmon and Cream Cheese Bagel
- Smoked Salmon Sushi Rolls
- Smoked Salmon and Spinach Quiche
- Smoked Salmon and Dill Potato Salad
- Smoked Salmon and Goat Cheese Tart
- Smoked Salmon Chowder
- Smoked Salmon and Cucumber Tea Sandwiches
- Smoked Salmon and Asparagus Frittata
- Smoked Salmon and Capers Crostini
- Smoked Salmon and Ricotta Pizza
- Smoked Salmon and Herb Omelet
- Smoked Salmon and Leek Risotto
- Smoked Salmon and Lemon Butter Linguine
- Smoked Salmon and Brie Panini
- Smoked Salmon Nicoise Salad
- Smoked Salmon Tartare with Avocado
- Smoked Salmon and Zucchini Fritters
- Smoked Salmon and Dill Cream Cheese Dip
- Smoked Salmon and Horseradish Canapés
- Smoked Salmon Pâté
- Smoked Salmon and Gruyère Tartlets
- Smoked Salmon and Roasted Beet Salad
- Smoked Salmon and Goat Cheese Stuffed Mushrooms
- Smoked Salmon and Artichoke Flatbread
- Smoked Salmon and Pomegranate Salad
- Smoked Salmon and Roquefort Bruschetta
- Smoked Salmon and Chive Deviled Eggs
- Smoked Salmon and Watercress Wraps
- Smoked Salmon and Avocado Sushi Bowl
- Smoked Salmon and Dill Butter on Rye
- Smoked Salmon and Apple Slaw
- Smoked Salmon and Lemon Dill Dressing Pasta

- Smoked Salmon and Wild Rice Salad
- Smoked Salmon and Gorgonzola Crostini
- Smoked Salmon and Red Onion Tart
- Smoked Salmon and Creamy Caper Dressing Salad
- Smoked Salmon and Tzatziki Wrap
- Smoked Salmon and Mango Salsa
- Smoked Salmon and White Wine Cream Sauce Fish
- Smoked Salmon and Sour Cream Pancakes
- Smoked Salmon and Spinach Stuffed Peppers
- Smoked Salmon and Sun-Dried Tomato Pesto Pasta
- Smoked Salmon and Caramelized Onion Galette
- Smoked Salmon and Herb Butter Croissant
- Smoked Salmon and Celeriac Remoulade
- Smoked Salmon and Lemon Dill Rice Bowl
- Smoked Salmon and Roasted Garlic Aioli Dip

Smoked Salmon Eggs Benedict

Ingredients:

For the Hollandaise Sauce:

- 3 large egg yolks
- 1 tbsp lemon juice
- ½ cup unsalted butter, melted
- 1 tsp Dijon mustard
- Salt and cayenne pepper to taste

For the Benedict:

- 2 English muffins, split and toasted
- 4 oz smoked salmon
- 4 large eggs
- 1 tbsp white vinegar
- Fresh dill or chives for garnish
- Salt and black pepper to taste

Instructions:

1. **Make the Hollandaise Sauce:**
    - In a heatproof bowl, whisk egg yolks and lemon juice until smooth.
    - Place the bowl over a saucepan with simmering water (do not let the bottom touch the water).
    - Slowly drizzle in the melted butter while whisking constantly until the sauce thickens.
    - Remove from heat, stir in Dijon mustard, season with salt and cayenne, and set aside.
2. **Poach the Eggs:**
    - Fill a saucepan with water and bring to a gentle simmer. Add vinegar.
    - Crack each egg into a small bowl and carefully slide it into the water.
    - Poach for about 3–4 minutes until the whites are set but yolks remain runny.
    - Remove with a slotted spoon and drain on a paper towel.
3. **Assemble the Benedict:**
    - Place toasted English muffin halves on plates.
    - Layer each half with smoked salmon slices.
    - Top with a poached egg.

- Drizzle with hollandaise sauce.
- Garnish with fresh dill or chives, and season with salt and black pepper.

Smoked Salmon and Avocado Toast

Ingredients:

- 2 slices sourdough or whole-grain bread, toasted
- 1 ripe avocado, mashed
- 4 oz smoked salmon
- 1 tbsp lemon juice
- ½ tsp red pepper flakes (optional)
- Salt and black pepper to taste
- Fresh dill or microgreens for garnish

Instructions:

1. Spread mashed avocado over toasted bread.
2. Drizzle with lemon juice and season with salt, black pepper, and red pepper flakes.
3. Top with smoked salmon.
4. Garnish with fresh dill or microgreens.
5. Serve immediately and enjoy!

Smoked Salmon Pasta with Cream Sauce

Ingredients:

- 8 oz pasta (fettuccine or linguine)
- 2 tbsp butter
- 2 cloves garlic, minced
- 1 cup heavy cream
- ½ cup grated Parmesan cheese
- 4 oz smoked salmon, chopped
- 1 tbsp lemon juice
- ½ tsp black pepper
- 2 tbsp chopped chives or parsley

Instructions:

1. Cook pasta according to package instructions; drain and set aside.
2. In a pan, melt butter over medium heat and sauté garlic until fragrant.
3. Pour in heavy cream and bring to a simmer.
4. Stir in Parmesan cheese, lemon juice, and black pepper.
5. Add smoked salmon and cooked pasta, tossing to combine.
6. Garnish with chives or parsley and serve warm.

Smoked Salmon and Cream Cheese Bagel

Ingredients:

- 1 bagel, sliced and toasted
- 3 tbsp cream cheese
- 4 oz smoked salmon
- ½ small red onion, thinly sliced
- 1 tbsp capers
- 1 tsp lemon juice
- Fresh dill for garnish

Instructions:

1. Spread cream cheese over toasted bagel halves.
2. Layer with smoked salmon, red onion, and capers.
3. Drizzle with lemon juice and garnish with fresh dill.
4. Serve immediately.

Smoked Salmon Sushi Rolls

Ingredients:

- 2 cups sushi rice, cooked and seasoned with rice vinegar
- 4 sheets nori (seaweed)
- 6 oz smoked salmon
- ½ cucumber, julienned
- ½ avocado, sliced
- 1 tbsp sesame seeds
- Soy sauce, wasabi, and pickled ginger for serving

Instructions:

1. Lay a sheet of nori on a bamboo sushi mat.
2. Spread an even layer of sushi rice over the nori, leaving a 1-inch border.
3. Place smoked salmon, cucumber, and avocado along the center.
4. Carefully roll using the sushi mat, applying gentle pressure.
5. Slice into bite-sized pieces and sprinkle with sesame seeds.
6. Serve with soy sauce, wasabi, and pickled ginger.

Smoked Salmon and Spinach Quiche

Ingredients:

- 1 pre-made pie crust
- 4 large eggs
- 1 cup heavy cream
- 1 cup fresh spinach, chopped
- 4 oz smoked salmon, flaked
- ½ cup shredded Gruyère or Swiss cheese
- 1 tbsp fresh dill, chopped
- Salt and black pepper to taste

Instructions:

1. Preheat oven to 375°F (190°C).
2. Place the pie crust in a tart pan and pre-bake for 10 minutes.
3. In a bowl, whisk eggs, heavy cream, salt, and pepper.
4. Spread spinach, smoked salmon, and cheese over the crust.
5. Pour the egg mixture over the filling and sprinkle with dill.
6. Bake for 30–35 minutes until set. Cool slightly before slicing.

Smoked Salmon and Dill Potato Salad

Ingredients:

- 1 lb baby potatoes, halved
- 4 oz smoked salmon, chopped
- ½ cup sour cream
- ¼ cup mayonnaise
- 1 tbsp Dijon mustard
- 2 tbsp fresh dill, chopped
- ½ small red onion, finely chopped
- Salt and black pepper to taste

Instructions:

1. Boil potatoes until fork-tender, then drain and cool.
2. In a bowl, mix sour cream, mayonnaise, mustard, dill, salt, and pepper.
3. Add cooled potatoes, smoked salmon, and red onion. Toss to coat.
4. Chill for 30 minutes before serving.

Smoked Salmon and Goat Cheese Tart

Ingredients:

- 1 sheet puff pastry
- 4 oz goat cheese, softened
- 4 oz smoked salmon, sliced
- 1 tbsp lemon zest
- 2 tbsp fresh chives, chopped
- 1 egg, beaten (for egg wash)

Instructions:

1. Preheat oven to 375°F (190°C). Roll out puff pastry on a baking sheet.
2. Spread goat cheese evenly over the pastry, leaving a 1-inch border.
3. Arrange smoked salmon on top, then sprinkle with lemon zest and chives.
4. Brush edges with egg wash and bake for 20–25 minutes until golden.
5. Serve warm.

Smoked Salmon Chowder

Ingredients:

- 2 tbsp butter
- 1 small onion, diced
- 2 cloves garlic, minced
- 2 cups diced potatoes
- 3 cups chicken or vegetable broth
- 1 cup heavy cream
- 6 oz smoked salmon, flaked
- ½ cup corn kernels (optional)
- 1 tsp smoked paprika
- 2 tbsp fresh dill, chopped
- Salt and black pepper to taste

Instructions:

1. In a pot, melt butter and sauté onion and garlic until soft.
2. Add potatoes, broth, and paprika. Simmer until potatoes are tender.
3. Stir in heavy cream, smoked salmon, and corn. Cook for 5 minutes.
4. Season with salt, pepper, and dill. Serve warm.

Smoked Salmon and Cucumber Tea Sandwiches

Ingredients:

- 8 slices white or whole wheat bread
- 4 oz smoked salmon, thinly sliced
- ½ cucumber, thinly sliced
- 4 tbsp cream cheese
- 1 tbsp fresh dill, chopped
- 1 tbsp lemon juice

Instructions:

1. Mix cream cheese, lemon juice, and dill. Spread on bread slices.
2. Layer smoked salmon and cucumber slices on half the bread slices.
3. Top with the remaining bread, then cut into small triangles.
4. Serve chilled.

Smoked Salmon and Asparagus Frittata

Ingredients:

- 6 large eggs
- ¼ cup milk
- 1 cup asparagus, chopped
- 4 oz smoked salmon, flaked
- ½ cup feta cheese, crumbled
- 1 tbsp olive oil
- Salt and black pepper to taste

Instructions:

1. Preheat oven to 375°F (190°C).
2. In a bowl, whisk eggs, milk, salt, and pepper.
3. In an ovenproof skillet, sauté asparagus in olive oil for 3 minutes.
4. Add smoked salmon and pour the egg mixture over. Sprinkle with feta.
5. Cook for 3 minutes, then transfer to the oven. Bake for 15 minutes.

Smoked Salmon and Capers Crostini

Ingredients:

- 1 baguette, sliced and toasted
- 4 oz smoked salmon
- ½ cup cream cheese
- 1 tbsp capers
- 1 tbsp lemon juice
- 1 tbsp fresh dill, chopped

Instructions:

1. Spread cream cheese on toasted baguette slices.
2. Top with smoked salmon, capers, and a drizzle of lemon juice.
3. Garnish with fresh dill. Serve immediately.

Smoked Salmon and Ricotta Pizza

Ingredients:

- 1 pizza crust (pre-made or homemade)
- ½ cup ricotta cheese
- 4 oz smoked salmon, sliced
- ½ red onion, thinly sliced
- 1 tbsp capers
- 1 tbsp olive oil
- Fresh arugula for garnish

Instructions:

1. Preheat oven to 400°F (200°C).
2. Brush pizza crust with olive oil and bake for 5 minutes.
3. Spread ricotta cheese over the crust.
4. Add smoked salmon, red onion, and capers.
5. Bake for another 10 minutes. Garnish with arugula and serve.

Smoked Salmon and Herb Omelet

Ingredients:

- 3 large eggs
- 2 tbsp milk
- 4 oz smoked salmon, flaked
- 1 tbsp butter
- 2 tbsp fresh chives, chopped
- ½ tsp black pepper

Instructions:

1. Whisk eggs, milk, chives, and black pepper.
2. Heat butter in a non-stick pan and pour in the egg mixture.
3. Cook for 2 minutes, then add smoked salmon.
4. Fold the omelet and cook for another minute. Serve warm.

Smoked Salmon and Leek Risotto

Ingredients:

- 1 cup Arborio rice
- 3 cups chicken or vegetable broth
- 1 small leek, thinly sliced
- 4 oz smoked salmon, flaked
- ½ cup white wine
- ½ cup Parmesan cheese, grated
- 2 tbsp butter
- Salt and black pepper to taste

Instructions:

1. Heat butter in a pan and sauté leeks until soft.
2. Add Arborio rice and cook for 2 minutes.
3. Pour in white wine and let it absorb.
4. Gradually add broth, stirring until the rice is creamy.
5. Stir in smoked salmon and Parmesan cheese. Serve warm.

Smoked Salmon and Lemon Butter Linguine

Ingredients:

- 8 oz linguine
- 4 oz smoked salmon, chopped
- 3 tbsp unsalted butter
- 2 cloves garlic, minced
- Zest and juice of 1 lemon
- ¼ cup heavy cream
- ¼ cup grated Parmesan cheese
- 2 tbsp fresh dill, chopped
- Salt and black pepper to taste

Instructions:

1. Cook linguine according to package instructions. Drain and set aside.
2. In a pan, melt butter and sauté garlic until fragrant.
3. Add lemon zest, lemon juice, and heavy cream. Stir until combined.
4. Toss in cooked pasta, smoked salmon, and Parmesan cheese.
5. Season with salt and black pepper. Garnish with fresh dill.

Smoked Salmon and Brie Panini

Ingredients:

- 2 ciabatta or sourdough bread slices
- 4 oz smoked salmon
- 2 oz Brie cheese, sliced
- 1 tbsp Dijon mustard
- 1 tbsp butter
- Handful of arugula

Instructions:

1. Spread Dijon mustard on one side of the bread.
2. Layer Brie cheese, smoked salmon, and arugula.
3. Close sandwich and butter the outside of the bread.
4. Grill in a panini press or on a skillet until golden brown.

Smoked Salmon Niçoise Salad

Ingredients:

- 4 oz smoked salmon
- 4 small potatoes, boiled and halved
- 1 cup green beans, blanched
- 2 hard-boiled eggs, halved
- ½ cup cherry tomatoes, halved
- ¼ cup black olives
- 2 tbsp olive oil
- 1 tbsp lemon juice
- 1 tsp Dijon mustard
- Salt and pepper to taste

Instructions:

1. Arrange all ingredients on a plate.
2. Whisk together olive oil, lemon juice, mustard, salt, and pepper.
3. Drizzle dressing over the salad. Serve fresh.

Smoked Salmon Tartare with Avocado

Ingredients:

- 4 oz smoked salmon, finely chopped
- 1 ripe avocado, diced
- 1 tbsp lemon juice
- 1 tbsp olive oil
- 1 tbsp capers, chopped
- 1 tbsp fresh chives, chopped
- Salt and black pepper to taste

Instructions:

1. In a bowl, mix smoked salmon, avocado, lemon juice, olive oil, capers, and chives.
2. Season with salt and pepper.
3. Serve in a ring mold or small dish for presentation.

Smoked Salmon and Zucchini Fritters

Ingredients:

- 1 zucchini, grated
- 4 oz smoked salmon, chopped
- ½ cup flour
- 1 egg
- 2 tbsp fresh dill, chopped
- 2 tbsp olive oil
- Salt and pepper to taste

Instructions:

1. Squeeze out excess moisture from grated zucchini.
2. Mix zucchini, flour, egg, smoked salmon, and dill.
3. Heat oil in a pan and fry small scoops until golden.
4. Serve with sour cream or yogurt.

Smoked Salmon and Dill Cream Cheese Dip

Ingredients:

- 8 oz cream cheese, softened
- 4 oz smoked salmon, chopped
- 2 tbsp fresh dill, chopped
- 1 tbsp lemon juice
- 1 tsp Worcestershire sauce

Instructions:

1. Mix all ingredients in a bowl until smooth.
2. Chill for 30 minutes before serving.
3. Serve with crackers or fresh veggies.

Smoked Salmon and Horseradish Canapés

Ingredients:

- 12 small rye bread slices
- 4 oz smoked salmon
- ½ cup sour cream
- 1 tbsp horseradish
- 1 tbsp fresh chives, chopped

Instructions:

1. Mix sour cream and horseradish.
2. Spread on rye bread and top with smoked salmon.
3. Garnish with chives.

Smoked Salmon Pâté

Ingredients:

- 6 oz smoked salmon
- 4 oz cream cheese
- 2 tbsp lemon juice
- 1 tbsp capers
- 1 tbsp fresh dill, chopped

Instructions:

1. Blend all ingredients in a food processor until smooth.
2. Serve with crackers or baguette slices.

Smoked Salmon and Gruyère Tartlets

Ingredients:

- 12 mini tart shells
- 4 oz smoked salmon, chopped
- ½ cup Gruyère cheese, shredded
- 1 egg
- ¼ cup heavy cream
- 1 tbsp fresh chives, chopped

Instructions:

1. Preheat oven to 375°F (190°C).
2. Mix egg, cream, and Gruyère cheese.
3. Fill tart shells with smoked salmon and pour egg mixture over.
4. Bake for 15 minutes. Garnish with chives.

Smoked Salmon and Roasted Beet Salad

Ingredients:

- 4 oz smoked salmon
- 1 roasted beet, sliced
- 2 cups arugula
- ¼ cup goat cheese, crumbled
- 2 tbsp walnuts, chopped
- 2 tbsp balsamic vinaigrette

Instructions:

1. Arrange arugula, beets, smoked salmon, goat cheese, and walnuts.
2. Drizzle with balsamic vinaigrette.

Smoked Salmon and Goat Cheese Stuffed Mushrooms

Ingredients:

- 12 large mushrooms, stems removed
- 4 oz goat cheese
- 4 oz smoked salmon, chopped
- 1 tbsp fresh chives, chopped

Instructions:

1. Preheat oven to 375°F (190°C).
2. Mix goat cheese, smoked salmon, and chives.
3. Stuff mushrooms with the mixture.
4. Bake for 15 minutes until tender.

Smoked Salmon and Artichoke Flatbread

Ingredients:

- 1 flatbread or naan
- 4 oz smoked salmon, chopped
- ½ cup marinated artichokes, drained and chopped
- ½ cup mozzarella cheese, shredded
- ¼ cup red onion, thinly sliced
- 2 tbsp cream cheese, softened
- 1 tbsp capers
- 1 tbsp fresh dill, chopped

Instructions:

1. Preheat oven to 400°F (200°C).
2. Spread cream cheese over the flatbread.
3. Top with mozzarella, artichokes, and red onion.
4. Bake for 10 minutes until crispy.
5. Add smoked salmon, capers, and dill before serving.

Smoked Salmon and Pomegranate Salad

Ingredients:

- 4 oz smoked salmon
- 4 cups mixed greens
- ¼ cup pomegranate seeds
- ¼ cup feta cheese, crumbled
- 2 tbsp walnuts, chopped
- 2 tbsp balsamic vinaigrette

Instructions:

1. Arrange greens, smoked salmon, pomegranate seeds, feta, and walnuts on a plate.
2. Drizzle with balsamic vinaigrette.

Smoked Salmon and Roquefort Bruschetta

Ingredients:

- 1 baguette, sliced
- 4 oz smoked salmon
- 2 oz Roquefort cheese
- 1 tbsp honey
- 1 tbsp walnuts, chopped

Instructions:

1. Toast baguette slices until golden.
2. Spread Roquefort cheese on each slice.
3. Top with smoked salmon, honey drizzle, and walnuts.

Smoked Salmon and Chive Deviled Eggs

Ingredients:

- 6 hard-boiled eggs, halved
- 4 oz smoked salmon, finely chopped
- ¼ cup mayonnaise
- 1 tbsp Dijon mustard
- 1 tbsp fresh chives, chopped
    - Salt and pepper to taste

Instructions:

1. Scoop out yolks and mash with mayonnaise, mustard, and chives.
2. Fold in smoked salmon.
3. Spoon mixture back into egg whites and garnish with extra chives.

Smoked Salmon and Watercress Wraps

Ingredients:

- 2 whole wheat wraps
- 4 oz smoked salmon
- 1 cup watercress
- 2 tbsp cream cheese
- 1 tbsp lemon juice

Instructions:

1. Spread cream cheese over each wrap.
2. Add smoked salmon, watercress, and a drizzle of lemon juice.
3. Roll tightly and slice into pinwheels or halves.

Smoked Salmon and Avocado Sushi Bowl

Ingredients:

- 1 cup sushi rice, cooked
- 4 oz smoked salmon, chopped
- 1 avocado, diced
- ½ cucumber, julienned
- 1 tbsp sesame seeds
- 1 tbsp soy sauce
- 1 tsp wasabi (optional)

Instructions:

1. Arrange rice in a bowl.
2. Top with smoked salmon, avocado, cucumber, and sesame seeds.
3. Drizzle with soy sauce and serve with wasabi.

Smoked Salmon and Dill Butter on Rye

Ingredients:

- 2 slices rye bread
- 4 oz smoked salmon
- 2 tbsp unsalted butter, softened
- 1 tbsp fresh dill, chopped
- 1 tsp lemon zest

Instructions:

1. Mix butter, dill, and lemon zest.
2. Spread over rye bread slices.
3. Top with smoked salmon and serve.

Smoked Salmon and Apple Slaw

Ingredients:

- 4 oz smoked salmon
- 1 apple, julienned
- 1 cup shredded cabbage
- ¼ cup Greek yogurt
- 1 tbsp apple cider vinegar
- 1 tsp honey

Instructions:

1. Mix cabbage, apple, Greek yogurt, vinegar, and honey.
2. Add smoked salmon and toss lightly.

Smoked Salmon and Lemon Dill Dressing Pasta

Ingredients:

- 8 oz pasta of choice
- 4 oz smoked salmon
- ¼ cup olive oil
- Juice of 1 lemon
- 1 tbsp Dijon mustard
- 2 tbsp fresh dill, chopped
- Salt and pepper to taste

Instructions:

1. Cook pasta and drain.
2. Whisk olive oil, lemon juice, mustard, dill, salt, and pepper.
3. Toss pasta with dressing and smoked salmon.

Smoked Salmon and Wild Rice Salad

Ingredients:

- 1 cup cooked wild rice
- 4 oz smoked salmon, chopped
- ¼ cup dried cranberries
- ¼ cup chopped pecans
- 2 tbsp olive oil
- 1 tbsp balsamic vinegar
- 1 tbsp fresh parsley, chopped

Instructions:

1. Mix all ingredients in a bowl.
2. Drizzle with olive oil and balsamic vinegar before serving.

Smoked Salmon and Gorgonzola Crostini

Ingredients:

- 1 baguette, sliced
- 4 oz smoked salmon
- 3 oz Gorgonzola cheese
- 1 tbsp honey
- 1 tbsp walnuts, chopped

Instructions:

1. Toast baguette slices until golden.
2. Spread Gorgonzola cheese on each slice.
3. Top with smoked salmon, honey drizzle, and chopped walnuts.

Smoked Salmon and Red Onion Tart

Ingredients:

- 1 sheet puff pastry
- 4 oz smoked salmon
- 1 small red onion, thinly sliced
- ½ cup crème fraîche
- 1 tbsp capers
- 1 tbsp fresh dill, chopped

Instructions:

1. Preheat oven to 375°F (190°C).
2. Roll out puff pastry and place on a baking sheet.
3. Spread crème fraîche over pastry and top with red onion slices.
4. Bake for 15 minutes until golden.
5. Top with smoked salmon, capers, and dill before serving.

Smoked Salmon and Creamy Caper Dressing Salad

Ingredients:

- 4 oz smoked salmon
- 4 cups mixed greens
- ¼ cup cherry tomatoes, halved
- ¼ cup cucumber, sliced
- 2 tbsp capers
- ¼ cup Greek yogurt
- 1 tbsp lemon juice
- 1 tbsp olive oil

Instructions:

1. Whisk yogurt, lemon juice, olive oil, and capers for dressing.
2. Toss greens, tomatoes, cucumber, and smoked salmon.
3. Drizzle with dressing and serve.

Smoked Salmon and Tzatziki Wrap

Ingredients:

- 2 whole wheat wraps
- 4 oz smoked salmon
- ½ cup tzatziki sauce
- ½ cucumber, julienned
- 1 tbsp fresh mint, chopped

Instructions:

1. Spread tzatziki over each wrap.
2. Add smoked salmon, cucumber, and mint.
3. Roll tightly and slice into halves or pinwheels.

Smoked Salmon and Mango Salsa

Ingredients:

- 4 oz smoked salmon, diced
- 1 mango, diced
- ¼ red onion, finely chopped
- 1 tbsp lime juice
- 1 tbsp cilantro, chopped

Instructions:

1. Mix mango, red onion, lime juice, and cilantro.
2. Add smoked salmon and gently toss.
3. Serve as a dip or topping for crackers.

Smoked Salmon and White Wine Cream Sauce Fish

Ingredients:

- 2 fillets of white fish (cod, halibut, or sole)
- 4 oz smoked salmon, chopped
- ½ cup heavy cream
- ½ cup white wine
- 1 tbsp butter
- 1 tbsp fresh dill

Instructions:

1. In a pan, melt butter over medium heat and cook fish fillets.
2. Remove fish and deglaze the pan with white wine.
3. Stir in heavy cream, smoked salmon, and dill, simmering until thickened.
4. Pour sauce over fish and serve.

Smoked Salmon and Sour Cream Pancakes

Ingredients:

- 1 cup all-purpose flour
- 1 tsp baking powder
- ½ tsp salt
- 1 cup milk
- ¼ cup sour cream
- 1 egg
- 4 oz smoked salmon, chopped
- 1 tbsp chives, chopped

Instructions:

1. Whisk flour, baking powder, and salt.
2. Stir in milk, sour cream, and egg until combined.
3. Fold in smoked salmon and chives.
4. Cook pancakes on a greased pan over medium heat.

Smoked Salmon and Spinach Stuffed Peppers

Ingredients:

- 2 large bell peppers, halved and seeded
- 4 oz smoked salmon, chopped
- 1 cup fresh spinach, chopped
- ½ cup cream cheese
- ¼ cup feta cheese, crumbled
- 1 tbsp lemon juice

Instructions:

1. Preheat oven to 375°F (190°C).
2. Mix smoked salmon, spinach, cream cheese, feta, and lemon juice.
3. Stuff mixture into bell peppers and bake for 20 minutes.

Smoked Salmon and Sun-Dried Tomato Pesto Pasta

Ingredients:

- 8 oz pasta (linguine or penne)
- 4 oz smoked salmon, chopped
- ¼ cup sun-dried tomatoes, chopped
- ¼ cup basil pesto
- ¼ cup heavy cream
- 2 tbsp olive oil
- 2 tbsp Parmesan cheese

Instructions:

1. Cook pasta according to package instructions.
2. In a pan, heat olive oil and sauté sun-dried tomatoes for 1-2 minutes.
3. Add pesto and heavy cream, stirring to combine.
4. Toss in cooked pasta and smoked salmon.
5. Serve topped with Parmesan.

Smoked Salmon and Caramelized Onion Galette

Ingredients:

- 1 sheet puff pastry
- 4 oz smoked salmon
- 2 large onions, thinly sliced
- 2 tbsp butter
- ¼ cup crème fraîche
- 1 tbsp capers
- 1 tsp fresh thyme

Instructions:

1. Preheat oven to 375°F (190°C).
2. In a pan, melt butter and cook onions until caramelized.
3. Roll out puff pastry and spread crème fraîche on top.
4. Add caramelized onions and bake for 15-18 minutes.
5. Top with smoked salmon, capers, and thyme before serving.

Smoked Salmon and Herb Butter Croissant

Ingredients:

- 2 croissants, sliced
- 4 oz smoked salmon
- 3 tbsp butter, softened
- 1 tbsp fresh dill, chopped
- 1 tbsp chives, chopped
- 1 tsp lemon zest

Instructions:

1. Mix butter with dill, chives, and lemon zest.
2. Spread herb butter inside each croissant.
3. Fill with smoked salmon and serve.

Smoked Salmon and Celeriac Remoulade

Ingredients:

- 1 small celeriac, peeled and julienned
- 4 oz smoked salmon, sliced
- ¼ cup mayonnaise
- 1 tbsp Dijon mustard
- 1 tbsp lemon juice
- 1 tbsp capers
- 1 tbsp parsley, chopped

Instructions:

1. Mix mayonnaise, mustard, lemon juice, and capers.
2. Toss with julienned celeriac and let sit for 10 minutes.
3. Serve with smoked salmon on top, garnished with parsley.

Smoked Salmon and Lemon Dill Rice Bowl

Ingredients:

- 1 cup cooked rice (white, brown, or jasmine)
- 4 oz smoked salmon
- 1 tbsp fresh dill, chopped
- 1 tbsp lemon juice
- 1 tbsp olive oil
- ¼ cup cucumber, sliced
- ¼ avocado, sliced

Instructions:

1. Drizzle olive oil and lemon juice over warm rice.
2. Top with smoked salmon, cucumber, and avocado.
3. Garnish with fresh dill before serving.

Smoked Salmon and Roasted Garlic Aioli Dip

Ingredients:

- 4 oz smoked salmon, finely chopped
- 1 head garlic, roasted
- ½ cup mayonnaise
- 1 tbsp lemon juice
- 1 tbsp fresh dill, chopped
- 1 tsp Dijon mustard

Instructions:

1. Mash roasted garlic and mix with mayonnaise, lemon juice, mustard, and dill.
2. Fold in smoked salmon.
3. Serve as a dip with crackers or toasted baguette slices.